Fix it, Fox

Written by Samantha Montgomerie
Illustrated by Gustavo Mazali

Collins

Fox can fix things.

He has a van.

Fox zips to this shop.

He chops.

Fox zigzags to Yak.

He bangs.

Can Fox get up ...

on this rock?

Bang!

Yak can fix the van.

Fox thanks Yak.

Fox can zip!

14

/y/

After reading

Letters and Sounds: Phase 3

Word count: 40

Focus phonemes: /v/ /x/ /y/ /z/ /qu/ /ch/ /sh/ /th/ /ng/ /nk/

Common exception words: to, the, he

Curriculum links: Personal, Social and Emotional development

Early learning goals: Reading: read and understand simple sentences; use phonic knowledge to decode regular words and read them aloud accurately; read some common irregular words

Developing fluency

- Your child may enjoy hearing you read the book.
- Ask your child to read pages 8 and 9, pausing for the ellipsis to add suspense, and using expression to make it sound like a question.

Phonic practice

- Focus on the words in which one sound is made up of two or more letters.
- Ask your child to sound out and blend the following:

  th/i/ng/s   sh/o/p   ch/o/p/s   b/a/ng/s   r/o/ck   th/a/nk/s
- Say the words and challenge your child to spell them out loud.
- Look at the "I spy sounds" pages (14–15). Take turns to find a word in the picture containing an /x/ or /y/ sound. (e.g. *six, box, axe, xylophone, yawn, yo-yo, yacht, yak, yolk, yoghurt*)

Extending vocabulary

- Check your child understands each of the verbs in the book.
- Ask your child to find the verbs in the book that are similar in meaning to:

  cuts (*chops*)   whizzes (*zips*)   hits (*bangs*)   mend (*fix*)
- Discuss phrases you could use instead of **zigzags** on page 6. (e.g. *twists up the road, snakes along, winds along the road, goes along the bendy road*)